TE DUE

The Shawnee Indians

by Joanne Mattern

Consultant:
James Squirrel, Chairman
Mary Mead, Shawnee Language Coordinator and Council Member
Loyal Shawnee Tribe

Bridgestone Books
an imprint of Capstone Press
Mankato, Minnesota

Bridgestone Books are published by Capstone Press
151 Good Counsel Drive, P.O. Box 669, Mankato, Minnesota 56002
http://www.capstone-press.com

Library of Congress Cataloging-in-Publication Data
Mattern, Joanne, 1963–
    The Shawnee Indians/by Joanne Mattern.
    p. cm.—(Native peoples)
    Includes bibliographical references and index.
    ISBN 0-7368-0833-7
    1. Shawnee Indians—Juvenile literature. [1. Shawnee Indians. 2. Indians of North
America—East (U.S.)] I. Title. II. Series.
E99.S35 M37 2001
973'.04973—dc21
                                                            00-009809

Summary: An overview of the past and present lives of the Shawnee Indians, including
their history, food and clothing, homes and family life, religion, and government.

Editorial Credits
Rebecca Glaser, editor; Karen Risch, product planning editor; Timothy Halldin, cover
    designer; Heather Kindseth, production designer; Linda Clavel, illustrator; Heidi Schoof,
    photo researcher

Photo Credits
Denver Public Library/Western History Collection, 8
Susan Thomas Underwood, cover, 6, 10, 12, 14, 18, 20
Unicorn Stock Photos/Richard B. Dippold, 16

1 2 3 4 5 6 06 05 04 03 02 01

Table of Contents

Canada

United States

Mexico

Traditional Location

The Shawnee originally lived in the forests of the
northeastern United States. They made their homes
along the Cumberland, Ohio, and Tennessee Rivers.
Today, most Shawnee live in Oklahoma.

Fast Facts

The Shawnee were once an Eastern Woodland tribe. Today, three Shawnee bands live in Oklahoma. These facts tell about the Shawnee in the past and present.

Homes: The Shawnee once made lodges from tree poles covered with bark or animal skins. Today, the Shawnee live in modern wood houses.

Food: In the past, Shawnee women planted crops such as corn, squash, beans, and sweet potatoes. Shawnee men fished, hunted, and set traps to catch animals. Today, the Shawnee buy food in supermarkets.

Clothing: Long ago, the Shawnee wore deerskin clothing. Men dressed in shirts and leggings. Women wore shirts and skirts. The Shawnee decorated clothing with beads, porcupine quills, and feathers. Today, the Shawnee wear clothing like that of other North Americans. They wear traditional clothing for celebrations and ceremonies.

Language: Shawnee is an Algonquian language. American Indians who lived in eastern North America spoke Algonquian languages. Shawnee still is spoken by some tribal elders and is used in ceremonies. Today, most young Shawnee speak only English.

The Shawnee People

Long ago, the Shawnee lived in the forests of northeastern North America. They were an Eastern Woodland tribe. The name Shawnee comes from the Algonquian word sawanwa. This word means "person of the south." The Shawnee received their name because they lived farther south than other Eastern Woodland tribes.

The Shawnee moved when the seasons changed to find food. During the summer, they lived farther north and planted crops. After the fall harvest, they moved to warmer valleys in the south for the winter.

Today, there are three Shawnee bands in the United States. The U.S. government recognizes two of the bands. The Absentee Shawnee's headquarters and the Eastern Shawnee's headquarters are in Oklahoma. The Loyal Shawnee live on Cherokee land in Oklahoma. The Loyal Shawnee are applying to the U.S. government for recognition.

Families camp together during tribal events.

Tecumseh

In the early 1800s, a young Shawnee chief named Tecumseh tried to unite the Eastern Woodland tribes against the United States. He wanted to save Shawnee land. Tecumseh's brother, Tenskwatawa, joined him. Tenskwatawa called himself "the Shawnee Prophet." He traveled to many villages to spread the word about Tecumseh's plans.

Tecumseh visited every tribe between the Great Lakes and Florida. While he was on this trip, Major General William Henry Harrison forced a group of chiefs to sell 3 million acres (1.2 million hectares) of land to the United States.

Tecumseh later fought with the British against the United States in the War of 1812 (1812–1814). In 1813, Tecumseh was killed in battle near the Thames River in Ontario, Canada. His death ended the movement to unite the Eastern Woodland tribes.

Shawnee History

The Shawnee once lived in the Cumberland and Ohio River valleys. They traveled throughout the eastern United States. Many of their villages were in present-day Ohio, Kentucky, and Tennessee.

In the 1700s, Europeans began to arrive in the northeastern woodlands. They settled on Shawnee land. The Europeans and the Shawnee fought many battles about land.

In 1795, the U.S. government forced the Shawnee and other American Indians to sign the Treaty of Greenville. This agreement gave parts of Ohio and Indiana to the United States. The United States also received the regions that are now the cities of Chicago and Detroit.

In 1830, the U.S. Congress passed the Indian Removal Act. This law forced all American Indians to move west of the Mississippi River. The Shawnee moved to Oklahoma and Kansas.

Homes, Food, and Clothing

Shawnee women built lodges called wigiwas from tree poles covered with bark or animal skins. In the summer, the Shawnee lived in rectangular-shaped lodges. Winter lodges were round and had domed roofs. These lodges were easier to heat.

The Shawnee once farmed and hunted for food. Women planted corn, squash, beans, and sweet potatoes. They gathered nuts and berries. Women made maple sugar from tree sap. Men hunted buffalo and deer. They also fished and set traps for rabbits, foxes, and other small animals.

The Shawnee once made deerskin clothing. Men wore shirts and leggings. Women dressed in shirts and skirts. Deerskin moccasins protected the Shawnee's feet. The Shawnee dyed their clothing bright colors. They decorated it with beads, porcupine quills, and feathers. The Shawnee still wear traditional clothing for celebrations. But their everyday clothing is like that of other North Americans.

Shawnee lodges, or wigiwas, were covered with bark. Winter lodges were round with domed roofs.

The Shawnee Family

Shawnee bands are divided into smaller groups of related families called clans. Each clan is named after an animal. Some clans today are Horse, Turtle, Wolf, and Chicken. The Shawnee believe that a clan's animal will protect it. Some Shawnee are known by both a personal name and a clan name.

In the past, every Shawnee family member had a job. Women farmed and gathered food. They also made baskets, clothing, and crafts. Men hunted, trapped, fished, and defended their tribe in battle. Grandparents, aunts, uncles, cousins, and in-laws lived near each other. Older members of the tribe taught younger members the Shawnee way of life. Girls worked with their grandmothers. Boys worked with their grandfathers.

Today, Shawnee families live like many other North American families. Adults work on ranches and farms, in offices, factories, stores, and at other jobs. Children go to school.

Shawnee families enjoy celebrating traditional events.

The Loyal Shawnee have a tribal business council.

Shawnee Government

In the past, the Shawnee did not have written laws. Instead, they followed a strict code of right and wrong. Every Shawnee was expected to be honest and loyal.

Each Shawnee band had at least one chief. War chiefs planned and led attacks against enemies. Peace chiefs directed tribal ceremonies and were in charge of health and food. Chiefs also served as judges. A chief's word was law. Other tribal members ignored people who did not accept a chief's punishment.

Tribal councils made decisions on important matters facing the tribe. Older members who had wisdom and experience served on councils.

Today, each Shawnee band has its own government of elected officials. The Absentee Shawnee have a governor. A chief is the head of the Eastern Shawnee tribe. A chairman or chief leads the Loyal Shawnee.

Shawnee Beliefs

The Shawnee believe in a Great Spirit who rules all of nature. They believe that all things in nature are sacred, or holy. The Shawnee hold ceremonies to honor the spirits. The Shawnee chant, pray, and dance to ask the spirits' help. The Shawnee also believe in a female creator called Kohkumthena, or "Our Grandmother."

Shawnee children go through the Green Snake Ceremony at age 3 or 4. During this ceremony, the head of a green snake is placed in the child's mouth for a few seconds. The Shawnee believe this brings the child good luck. The Shawnee perform this ceremony so their children will have good health as they grow up.

Today, some Shawnee follow Christianity or other religions. But they also hold traditional dances to honor the spirits. Tribal headquarters have grounds and a lodge for dances. Shawnee members travel great distances to take part in tribal dances.

The Shawnee believe that green snakes bring good luck.

A Shawnee Legend

The Shawnee creation legend says that Kohkumthena created the Shawnee and taught them how to live and work. She also gave her children a set of rules to follow.

Kohkumthena then went up to her heavenly home. She still sits there and weaves a basket. She watches her Earth children from a window in the sky. Kohkumthena will gather the Shawnee people into the basket when it is finished. She will take them up to heaven to live with her.

But Kohkumthena is never able to finish weaving her basket. Her grandson, Cloudy Boy, and her little dog always undo the weaving during the night. That is why Our Grandmother has not yet returned to collect her people.

Shawnee artist Susan Thomas Underwood painted this picture of the spirit Kohkumthena, or "Our Grandmother," blessing a mother and a child.

Seasonal Dances

The Shawnee held dances each year to celebrate the seasons. They gave thanks and prayed to the Creator during these dances. The dances still take place today.

The Shawnee held the Spring Bread Dance to honor the women who planted crops. People asked the Creator for a good growing season. The Shawnee played a ceremonial ball game to bring rain for the crops. The men played against the women. The teams tried to kick a deerskin ball into a goal.

Each summer, the Shawnee held the Green Corn Dance to celebrate the growing corn. During this ceremony, the Shawnee thanked the Creator for the first crops of the season. The Shawnee also named new babies at this time. Only the Loyal Shawnee hold the Green Corn Dance today.

At harvest time, the Shawnee held the Fall Bread Dance. This ceremony honored the men who hunted for the tribe. The Fall Bread Dance also was a time to thank the Creator for a successful harvest.

This painting by Susan Thomas Underwood shows Shawnee people preparing for a ceremony.

Hands On: Make a Beaded Necklace

The Shawnee are well known for the beautiful beaded designs they create. The Shawnee still make beaded jewelry, clothes, belts, and hats.

What You Need

Lanyard or leather strip, about 18 inches (46 centimeters) long
Beads of different sizes, colors, and shapes

What You Do

1. Sort your beads into groups of the same colors, shapes, and sizes.
2. Decide the pattern your necklace will have.
3. Tie a knot in one end of the lanyard. Leave a 1-inch (2.5-centimeter) "tail" behind the knot.
4. String the beads on the lanyard, following the pattern you created.
5. Tie a knot in other end of the lanyard. Leave a 1-inch (2.5-centimeter) "tail" at the end.
6. Tie the "tails" together to complete your necklace.

Words to Know

clan (KLAN)—a group of related families
prophet (PROF-it)—someone who predicts the future
sawanwa (sah-WAHN-wah)—an Algonquian word meaning "person of the south"
territory (TER-uh-tor-ee)—a large area of land
treaty (TREE-tee)—a formal agreement between two or more nations
wigiwa (wee-GEE-wah)—a traditional Shawnee lodge built from tree poles covered with bark or animal skins

Read More

Flanagan, Alice K. *The Shawnee.* A True Book. New York: Children's Press, 1998.

Immell, Myra H. and William H. Immell. *Tecumseh.* The Importance of. San Diego: Lucent Books, 1997.

Landau, Elaine. *The Shawnee.* A First Book. New York: Franklin Watts, 1997.

Stefoff, Rebecca. *Tecumseh and the Shawnee Confederation.* Library of American Indian History. New York: Facts on File, 1998.

Useful Addresses

Absentee Shawnee Tribe
2025 S. Gordon Cooper
Shawnee, OK 74801

Eastern Shawnee Tribe
P.O. Box 350
Seneca, MO 64865

**Loyal Shawnee Tribe
   of Oklahoma**
P.O. Box 189
Miami, OK 74355

Internet Sites

Eastern Shawnee Tribe of Oklahoma
http://showcase.netins.net/web/shawnee/main.html
Native American, the Shawnee
http://www.merceronline.com/Native/native 02.htm

Index